THE GIANTS FAN'S
LITTLE BOOK OF WISDOM

THE GIANTS FAN'S
LITTLE BOOK OF WISDOM

David D'Antonio

Diamond Communications
A Member of the Rowman & Littlefield Publishing Group
Lanham • South Bend • New York • Oxford

THE GIANTS FAN'S LITTLE BOOK OF WISDOM

Copyright © 2002 by David D'Antonio

Manufactured in the United States of America

Published by Diamond Communications
An imprint of The Rowman & Littlefield Publishing Group, Inc.
4501 Forbes Boulevard, Suite 200
Lanham, Maryland 20706
Distributed by National Book Network
1-800-464-6420

ISBN   1-888698-34-9

• Introduction •

When you go to a Giants game at Pac Bell Park you must notice the family atmosphere. At times the family may seem dysfunctional, more Bundy than Brady, but it is family nonetheless. Dusty Baker is the wise father offering discipline, encouragement and unparalleled toothpick gymnastics. Robb Nen is the menacing and silent uncle that it's best to avoid, Marvin Benard the troubled kid brother that gets on everyone's nerves, Jeff Kent the independent middle child who can't keep off of his motorcycle, and Barry Bonds the I-can't-help-but-be-a-pain-in-the-behind brother who always wants his way—and usually gets it—while tormenting siblings and parents alike.

Parents? Yes, yes, I said parents. Admittedly it's hard to come up with maternal figures on most teams (what a pity that neither Gene Brabender nor Lady Baldwin ever pitched for San Francisco), but the Giants fortunately have Mike Krukow in the broadcasting booth. Kruk's relentless enthusiasm, welcoming entreaties, and ready advice for any moment make for the ideal Mom. A string of pearls, a can of corn, and, presto, June Cleaver with a curve.

As for the 2.5 million fans, well, consider us neighbors, part of the family, who dropped in when we could, appreciated the hospitality, and inevitably left the place a mess.

And since we are family, we come together, share secrets, and ridicule each other like teammates, only occasionally to the point of tears. That's why I feel comfortable sharing my early morning habits.

For more than 30 years my days have started much the same way: I awake at 6, walk blurredly outside and grab the morning paper. (You could chart my transience by the papers I have grabbed over the years—*San Jose Mercury, Los Angeles Times, Washington Post, Modesto Bee, Sacramento Bee, Hayward Daily Review,* and *San Francisco Chronicle.*) I free the sports from the news sections, head to the bathroom, flip on the light, toss the sports to the floor, take a seat, and officially begin my day. My routine brings the most satisfaction from February to October when I read about the Giants, who are as close to my heart as porcelain is to another body part.

How many other childhood routines extend into adulthood? Maybe bedtime prayers, clandestine ways to avoid vegetable consumption, and appreciation for television reruns.

• INTRODUCTION •

In baseball, like in all great TV shows, we remember moments which we recount later, whether the next day or the next decade. Or in the case of my first baseball game, more than three decades later. Showing confidence in a world far different from today's, my mom drove my brother Ken, my best friend Rick, and me to a Santa Clara bus station. Ken, at 12 years old, was in charge. Rick was nine.

And I was eight, eager for the first adventure of my life, a 50-minute bus ride to Candlestick Park for an August double-header against the Mets. For a child who could and did get lost on his own street, the trip took on Everestian significance.

To say I fell in love that day isn't accurate. Love had started a year or two earlier during a Giants-Braves game I watched on TV. Jack Hiatt homered and became mighty. He was Babe Ruth in my eyes, although adult wisdom now tells me he more often hit like Ruth's Baby. But I don't care. He is always mighty—for that home run is my earliest baseball memory.

The romance deepened in my first year of Little League in 1968 when I played on—the National Anthem, please—the Giants. The world was perfect. It was a sign from God that all was well, that I would eventually play for the real Giants. Had I known what destiny meant I would have used the word because I surely felt it.

So when I arrived at Candlestick with Ken and Rick, love was already as present as the Rick Monday glove I clutched. The games that day, the games where Tom Seaver nearly killed Ron Hunt with a fastball off the head, where Bobby Bonds made a great throw to nail a runner at the plate, where Jimmy Davenport scored on a bases loaded walk, well, those games were like a first kiss: I was thrilled, breathless. I desired more; I didn't want the moment to end. But because I was only eight I knew nothing about first kisses and the complexity that follows them. 1969 was a great year to begin following the Giants. They were part of a 5-team race and I knew they would win their division.

They didn't. They finished second. This romance thing, I realized, might not be all hot dogs and soda pop after all. Next year would be different.

It was. They finished third.

In 1971, of course, the Giants won their division by a game over the Dodgers, who I learned to hate as easily as I read the sports page. Juan Marichal's 5-1 victory over San Diego clinched the title in the season's final game. I watched the final outs, bouncing anxiously on my parents' bed. I could tell Marichal was tiring, so I willed him my arm strength through the TV screen, an often overlooked detail in newspaper accounts of that game.

Pittsburgh was next, and when the Giants won the opener I'd never been happier. When the Pirates swept the next three games I felt the unique pain of playoff defeat.

But this was my family and you stick with them. Sure, you compare a little and sometimes complain a lot but you're with them through all situations, through broken fingers and birthday parties, through painful losses and magical seasons.

We rejoice and commiserate and remember the past: Darrell Evans smacking three home runs against Houston, each farther than the last; Fran Healy destroying the Cubs in a 1971 double-header; Will Clark smoking a bases loaded double in the ninth inning in a 7-6 victory; Ken Henderson homering off the foul pole; six straight hits against Greg Maddux!

We remember the Crazy Crab and Croix de Candlestick, Bud Black and Vida Blue. We smile at the silliness of Bob Burda, Bob Barton, Bob Bolin, and Bobby Bonds on the same team. We booed and Kazooed Lasorda and took for granted a lineup of Mays, Marichal, and McCovey. We saw Matt Williams' debut, cringed at his struggles, applauded his bat and glove and character, and cried when he left. And in our wildest moments Ernest Riles and Joel Youngblood enter our thoughts and we became 10 or 11 on a sunny day with a glove and unspoken dreams.

We listened to Russ and Lon and Hank and Jon and scores more. We read about the old-timers—Matty, Hubbell, Ott, McGraw, Dusty Rhodes, Monte Irvin, Whitey Lockman—and realize that the players of our childhood have joined them, and as we read we, as brothers and sisters, look toward tomorrow, for the next day, for the next season, for the next Giants game.

Dedication

To Joey,
My big brother

Enjoy the first time;
it may be the last.

In 1952, Hoyt Wilhelm homered in his first at bat in the
major leagues. During his 21-season career, a span which covered
another 431 official trips to the plate, he never hit another.

Choose your athletic supporters carefully.

The Giants' choice to throw out the first ball in the
first game at Candlestick Park in 1960 was
Vice President Richard Nixon. It was not reported whether
his toss was a trick pitch or if the ball sailed wide to the right.

Start your day with a balanced meal.

"[John] McGraw eats gunpowder every morning for breakfast and washes it down with warm blood."

—A National League umpire

Honor thy mother...
unless she's the winning run.

"Look, I'm playing third base. My mother's on second. The ball's hit to short center. As she goes by me on the way to third, I'll accidentally trip her up. I'll help her up, brush her off, tell her I'm sorry. But she doesn't get to third."

—Leo Durocher

Don't hurry God, and double check His answers.

"I'll pray on it, like I always do. I'll pray on it and ask the good Lord to help me make the right decision. I just wouldn't mind Him hurrying up."—Manager Dusty Baker seeking help in choosing his starting pitcher for the final game of the 1993 season when the Giants and Braves were tied at 103-58. Salomon Torres was the answer, but not the one San Francisco needed, as he took a 12-1 loss to, groan, the Dodgers.

Earn your keep.

Smiling Mickey Welch pitched complete games in his first 105
starts, played center field when he wasn't pitching, watched
the turnstiles before games, and would no doubt have sung
the National Anthem had tradition called for it in the 1880s.
His annual salary: $4,000.

Ignorance is bliss.

Wouldn't life as a Giants fan be easier if we had never heard of Cepeda for Sadecki, Foster for Duffy, Perry for McDowell, Bonds for Murcer, et al?

If at first you don't succeed, try touching second.

Poor Fred Merkle. His failure to touch second base against Chicago became baseball's biggest boner and cost the Giants the 1908 pennant. Merkle went on to a solid big league career, while the Cubs won the World Series. It should be noted, however, that Chicago hasn't won one since. Consider it Merkle's Revenge.

Watch what you eat.

"I reckon I tried everything on the old apple but salt
and pepper and chocolate sauce topping."—Gaylord Perry
on either his spitballing techniques or dietary habits

Watch what you say.

"Is Brooklyn still in the league?" The answer to player-manager
Bill Terry's question was, unfortunately, yes, as evidenced
by the Dodgers' late-season wins over the Giants, costing
them a share of the pennant.

Watch what you say (grammatically challenged division).

"The Giants is dead."—Dodger manager Charlie Dressen's mid-season coroner's report made before the Giants stormed from the coffin to take the 1951 pennant

The distance between a dream and a nightmare is 60'6".

Called up to the Giants on September 3, 1992, Kevin Rogers made his
debut a day later against the Cardinals and, on his first pitch
in the major leagues, gave up a home run to Geronimo Peña.

A bad start doesn't mean a bad day.

Playing third base on September 4, 1986, Bob Brenly tied a major league record with four errors in one inning, but countered his failures with two home runs against the Braves, including a game-winning blast on a 3-2 pitch with two outs in the bottom of the ninth.

Practice random acts of kindness.

The Giants and Yankees played the first major league Sunday game at the Polo Grounds—an exhibition contest on April 21, 1912— to aid survivors of the *Titanic*, which had sunk a week earlier. The crowd donated more than $9,000, prompting *The New York Times* to report, "The baseball fan has heart, just like anybody else, although often in the daily strife of the game, it is carefully hidden."

It's not what you say, it's how you say it.

Pitcher Dummy Taylor, a deaf mute who won 114 games
for the Giants from 1900-1909, was once
booted from a game for insulting umpire Hank O'Day.

Be creative in the grasp of adversity.

During a September 1986 game, the Mets' Keith Hernandez smacked a comebacker to Terry Mulholland, who could not remove the ball from his glove. Showing unusually quick thinking for a rookie (and a lefthander at that), Mulholland jogged toward first base and tossed his glove, with ball embedded, to Bob Brenly. Brenly, it should be noted, made the catch. (See No. 13)

Find the John Pregenzer in everyone.

John Pregenzer appeared in only 19 games for San Francisco in 1963 and '64, but his impact was so great that it seemed he had single-armedly pitched the Giants to the World Series. A fan club attracted President Kennedy, Charles Schulz, Joe Dimaggio, Helen Gurley Brown, and Norman Mailer as members, and a 50-foot banner hung proudly at Candlestick: "The Aim Of The John Pregenzer Fan Club Is To Make This A Better World For John Pregenzer To Pitch In."

To error is human...

The 1900 New York Giants squad committed 439 errors,
one-fifth of them by third baseman "Piano Legs" Hickman,
who was off-key 86 times.

…To forgive divine.

"Often I have been asked to tell what I did to Fred Snodgrass
after he dropped that fly ball in the World Series of 1912…
Well, I will tell you exactly what I did: I raised his salary $1,000."
—John McGraw, whose actions when employees
blunder is a must for all bosses, particularly mine

20

Have fun on the job.

On Turn Back the Clock Day in 1991, Matt Williams performed
a dead-on imitation of Babe Ruth's called shot, complete with
dramatic pointing, a Ruthian swing, those odd tiny steps the
Babe used, and a tummy seemingly created by hot dogs and beer.

Work toward
international understanding.

The Giants of the early 1960s led the league in Spanish-speaking players, which occasionally led to conflicts, including one dispute in Cincinnati with Orlando Cepeda on second base.
"Don't you know how to talk English?" snapped the Reds pitcher.
"Kiss my ass," Cepeda said. "Is that English enough for you?"

Get rid of on-the-job distractions.

"Pick up a handful of dirt and throw it in his face."
—Leo Durocher's advice to 19-year-old rookie Willie Mays
on how to stop Roy Campanella's needle-filled conversation
whenever Mays came to bat

Seek beauty.

"I think a baseball field must be the most beautiful
thing in the world. It's so honest and precise…Every
star gets humbled. Every mediocre player has a great moment."
—Jim Lefebvre

Don't settle for just a pretty face.

"If he could cook I'd marry him," said Leo Durocher about Willie Mays, while showing surprising openness for same sex marriage.

We have nothing to fear but beer itself.

Bugs Raymond was a good pitcher but a better drinker.
After three seasons with the Giants he couldn't stay
sober, leading to his release in 1911 and his death in 1912
at the age of 30.

Value your education.

Before the 1989 Bay Bridge World Series, a reporter asked Giants
manager Roger Craig whether the A's would have an advantage
because of Oakland manager Tony LaRussa's law degree. "I graduated
from high school," said the ever-optimistic Craig, who could
have used a lawyer after the A's assaulted his club in four straight games.

Speak softly and carry a big stick (but don't use it in a pennant race).

Juan Marichal was suspended for 10 days during the heat of the 1965 pennant race when he Louisville Sluggered Dodger catcher John Roseboro. Marichal felt Roseboro had tried to hit him with return throws to Sandy Koufax. The Giants' headache was perhaps worse than Roseboro's when they lost the pennant by two games.

Break barriers.

Sherry Davis became the first female public address announcer
in baseball history in 1993, 87 years after women were
first allowed to sell tickets at the Polo Grounds.

If you don't have anything nice to say…just eat and shut up.

Asked his thoughts on the Giants' pennant chances in 1927, second baseman Rogers Hornsby said, "Not with [Doc] Farrell at shortstop." The contentious Hornsby was eating with Farrell at the time.

Mama, don't let your sons grow up to be dictators.

Giants scouts expressed interest in signing a young Cuban right-hander named Fidel Castro, who instead hurled anti-Yankee invectives from the left in a lifetime career with the Reds.

Image is everything.

"He's old, bald and huge. He looks like he'd spend the rest of his God-given days as a couch potato. So play against his type. Have him smartly dressed and saying only X-brand tuxedo will do for a night on the town."—Advertising director Geoff Thompson explaining how to market pitcher Rick Reuschel, who typically showed as much charisma as the foul line

Prepare for rain.

So hated were the Giants that Brooklyn fans sharpened
umbrella tips into weapons and, from rooftop perches, rained
them upon Giant outfielders in the early 1900s.

Believe in yourself, even if statistics say not to.

After recovering from an injury, shortstop Blondy Ryan announced his return and encouraged his teammates with this July 11, 1933, telegram: "They cannot beat us. Am en route." Ryan had the team's lowest batting average at .238, but the Giants did win the World Series.

Everything is relative.

"This wouldn't be such a bad place to play if it wasn't for the wind.
I guess that's like saying hell wouldn't be such a bad place if it
wasn't for the heat."—Candlestick Park Critic Jerry Ruess, who
didn't complain when he no-hit the Giants at the 'Stick in 1980

Be grateful for the little things in life.

"Every time I sign a ball, and there must have been thousands, I thank my luck that I wasn't born Coveleski, or Wambsganns or Peckinpaugh."

—Mel Ott

Be honest with yourself…

Face it, as much as Hal Lanier frustrated you, you'd trade places with him in a second (or as long as it took him to kill a rally) for a taste, any taste, of his big league career.

…Unless you really have to lie.

"You must have an alibi to show why you lost. If you haven't one, you must fake one. Your self-confidence must be maintained."

—Christy Mathewson

Take chances.

In 1901, John McGraw tried to pass Charlie Grant,
a black infielder, as a Cherokee Indian named
Charlie Takahoma. The ploy was unsuccessful and
baseball's color barrier remained
unbroken for another 46 years.

Don't get pushed around.

"If someone says don't come out, you've got to come out.
You can't let someone punk you out in front of
50,000 people and a televised audience."—Eminently
hip Giants manager Dusty Baker explaining why he was
obligated to confront umpire Larry Vanover, who had told
him to stay put. Baker was ejected from the July 2, 1999,
game, but you had the feeling he didn't mind.

Put the interests of others ahead of your own.

Russ Hodges normally called the eighth and ninth innings of games, but when Juan Marichal had a no-hitter after 7, Hodges let Lon Simmons stay on the air. "I'm giving you a [birthday] present," Hodges told Simmons. "I've done no-hitters but you never have." And after the game, Simmons still hadn't, thanks to Clay Dalrymple's eighth-inning single.

Sometimes the least are last.

Johnnie LeMaster started the 1985 season in San Francisco,
where he hit .000 in 12 games when he was traded to Cleveland,
where he hit .150 in 11 games when he was shipped to Pittsburgh,
where he hit .155 in 22 games. Each team lost at least
100 games and finished in last place.

War is hell…

The first player to die in World War I was Harvard-educated
Giants infielder Eddie Grant, who was killed in the
Argonne Forest in France on October 5, 1918.
He was 35.

...And baseball is war.

After beaning the Braves' Joe Adcock, Ruben Gomez
did not care for the big first baseman's comments. Gomez
retrieved the ball and hit Adcock again. Adcock chased the
hot-headed Giants pitcher, who hot-footed it to the
clubhouse where he scooped up an ice pick.
He was tackled before he could use it.

Lift your friends up
when their spirits are down.

"You're my center fielder if you don't get a hit the rest of the season."
—Leo Durocher to Willie Mays, who, after starting his major
league career 0 for 12, begged to be removed from the lineup

"What the hell has happened to the pitching since I went away to the war?"

—General Dwight Eisenhower to Giants owner
Horace Stoneham, showing that, even with World War II
over, he still couldn't stop worrying about arms

If today is bleak, there's always yesterday.

"A Giant is a midget, gettin' by on his past,
He can't hit a hook, or nuthin' fast,
His club makes money, but it's gone to pot,
The fans go there to dream of Hubbell and Ott."
—popular 1946 verse about
the 61-93, last place Giants

Pay attention in school; it might come in handy.

"I wanted to be a surfer…I spent my first minor league season at Waterloo, Iowa. When I was assigned there, I thought, 'Great—Waterloo. It has to be near an ocean.' "
—Greg "Moon Man" Minton, who spent much of his time in the lunar realm and was only, oh, a thousand miles or so from the ocean for which he yearned

Don't let the weather get you down.

"If the wind would be blowing out, [Johnny] Mize would lie back in bed and puff that cigar and say, 'Roomie, I'm going to hit one or two today.' And he would. If the wind was blowing in, he'd come back to the bed and put out his cigar and just lie there."

—Bill Rigney

Don't take yourself too seriously.

Ed Bressoud's license plate read E-6 to commemorate a comment from a woman who recalled an error that shortstop Bressoud made in Juan Marichal's debut. In retrospect, it's a good thing he didn't get sick in the dugout or suffer from a runny nose.

Know when to quit.

Jackie Robinson retired rather than accept his trade to
the Giants. Unfortunately, Juan Marichal didn't pay attention
as he chose to end his career in 1975 with the Dodgers.
Fortunately, he lost his only decision.

You can't get too much of a good thing.

"The Giants win the pennant! The Giants win the pennant!
The Giants win the pennant! Bobby Thomson hits it into the
lower deck of the left field stands! The Giants win the pennant
and they're going crazy! They're going crazy!"
—Russ Hodges' call on The Shot Heard 'Round the World

52

"Baseball is like being a kid, and I hope I never grow up."

—Mike Sadek

There is, gulp, more to life than baseball.

According to *The Sporting Life* in 1888, 300-game winner Tim Keefe cloistered himself in his hotel room for hours each day, practicing "those mysterious twists and loops and arches and dots." Keefe was preparing for the day when his pitching arm was long gone; he was learning short-hand.

Take pride in your work.

Don Liddle pitched to one batter in Game 1 of the 1954
World Series. He gave up a 440-foot blast to Vic Wertz
which Willie Mays corralled in one of baseball's
most memorable catches. "I did my job," Liddle later said.

Don't make the same mistake twice.

On June 9, 1946, Mel Ott became the first manager to
be ejected from both games of a double-header. He was tossed
in the eighth inning of the opener and lasted only
until the fifth of the nightcap.

Be fruitful and multiply— and learn to count.

"They shouldn't throw at me. I'm the father of five or six kids."—Tito Fuentes

You can't please everybody.

When the Giants played their final game in New York on
September 27, 1957, before moving to San Francisco, fans
chanted their desire for Giants owner Horace Stoneham:

We want Stoneham.

We want Stoneham.

We want Stoneham

With a rope around his neck.

Trust your heart—love at first sight is the real thing…

Facing Robin Roberts in his major league debut in 1959, Willie McCovey went 4 for 4 with two triples en route to a career of Giant glory and memories.

…But remember that love can be foolish and the heart deceitful.

In 1971, Dave Kingman, playing in his second major league contest, replaced Willie McCovey early in the game and drove in five runs with a double and grand slam en route to a career of Giant disappointment and headaches.

Timing is everything.

"Look at the contrast in salaries between today and my day.
I wish my mama had better timing."
—Monte Irvin, whose mama gave birth to the future
Hall-of-Famer on February 25, 1919,
no doubt wished for the same thing

Dylan had it wrong, my friend.

News Item: Tiny Giant reliever Stu Miller was called for a balk
when a strong wind nudged him in the ninth inning of the
1961 All-Star Game at Candlestick Park.

Sung to the tune of *Blowin' In The Wind*

How many mounds must a man fall from before they call him a man?
How many times must a reliever balk before he can throw the next pitch?
How many times must the hurricanes fly before they're forever banned?
Stu Miller, my friend, is blowin' in the wind. Stu Miller is blowing in the wind.

Keep your home safe from theft.

When the Dodgers came to town in 1962, Giants groundskeeper
Matty Schwab watered the dirt around first base until he
created a swamp. The plot was to slow base thief champ
Maury Wills, but was noticed by do-gooding umpires who
demanded that Schwab add sand to the area. The result: an even
greater morass for Maury, and it clearly was not quick sand.

Remember the good 'ol days.

"Mr. McGraw was a product of the old school of baseball
when fist fights were common, when red liquor was sold at
all the parks, when only ladies of questionable social
standing attended the games."—*World-Telegram* reporter
Joe Williams, who would be right at home with the "old"
school of baseball still practiced at Yankee Stadium

Abstain from every form of evil…

—1 Thessalonians 5:22

Divine support that Dodger personnel and paraphanelia of any
type should be strictly avoided, if not quarantined and
purged, from respectable society.

…But look for the positive in everything.

The Brooklyn Dodgers of 1943 and '44 included a backup catcher by the name of Fats Dantonio, who was only an apostrophe and capital A short of greatness.

Love thy brother, Jesus says, and back him up if he errs.

The Alou brothers—Felipe, Matty, and Jesus—shared the outfield and each batted in the eighth inning in a 4-2 loss to the Mets. Jesus, leading off, grounded to short, Matty struck out, and Felipe ended the inning with a comebacker. Adieu, Alous.

Life isn't fair.

During the 1960s, Juan Marichal won 191 games and had six
seasons with more than 20 victories. He was one of baseball's
most dominating pitchers, yet he never won the Cy Young Award.
Teammate Mike McCormick won 78 games in the decade, including
22 in 1967 that gave him the Cy Young Award.

68

"Baseball must be a great game to survive the fools who run it."

—Bill Terry

Shoot for new frontiers.

After witnessing Gaylord Perry's futile swings in the batting cage, manager Alvin Dark predicted, "There'll be a man on the moon before he hits a home run." Years later, on July 20, 1969, Perry came to the plate against the Dodgers' Claude Osteen and launched his first major league home run. The Eagle's lunar landing had occurred 20 minutes earlier.

Follow orders but maintain your humor.

When told to shorten his pre-game show, Giants announcer
Hank Greenwald came on the air and said, "Hello,
everybody, and welcome to 2 Rivers Stadium in Pittsburgh."

Show your feminine side.

"(W)hen things begin to go wrong, he is a composite of ginger and bad language. In his clumsy shin guards and wind-pad, his head in a wire cage, through which at intervals comes a stream of reproof and comment as he fusses around the plate, he suggests a grotesque overgrown hen trying to get the family in out of the rain."—J. W. McConaughy on Hall-of-Fame catcher Roger Breshnahan

Sometimes crying is the only reasonable response.

During a 19-month period covering 1972 and 1973, the
Giants got rid of Willie Mays, Willie McCovey, and Juan Marichal.
In return they received Charlie Williams, Mike Caldwell,
some money, and, from their fans, tears and contempt.

For a maturing investment put your money in Bonds.

At 37, Barry Bonds had the best year of his life. He broke Mark McGwire's home run mark, smashed Babe Ruth's slugging percentage record, and modestly discussed his success: "You can't really explain it. I come around and touch home plate and I'm in the dugout, and I'm like, 'What the hell did I just do.' "

Even when you're not the best, on any given day you just might be.

Jim Barr ended his 12-year career with a 101-112 record, but on August 23 and 29 of 1972 he retired 41 consecutive batters, a mark that still stands.

"The two toughest things for a young player when he comes into baseball is to learn to eat right, and to marry the right girl."

—Bob Kennedy, Nutritionist, Matchmaker, and Giants Vice President

Seek input from your workers.

"Mr. Craig, where would you like me to position the right fielder?
In the upper deck or lower deck?"—Casey Stengel to Roger Craig
with Willie McCovey at the plate

"Ron, believe me, there's no advantage in turning my color."

—Bobby Bonds to Ron Hunt after yet another region of the Giants second baseman's body was blackened by a pitch

There is more to baseball than meets the eye.

Wanting his club to relax after losing six straight games in 1984, manager Frank Robinson brought in a stripper. "[S]he had glasses on, a straight back hairdo, wearing a suit, very business-like," said one player.

There's no sharing in baseball.

"When I'm pitching, I figure the plate is mine, and I
don't like anybody getting too close to it."
—Sal "The Barber" Maglie

Get it while the gettin's good.

Ken Oberkfell was the league's top pinch-hitter in 1989, and
whenever he returned to the dugout after a successful at bat,
he'd say, "Well, that's another $50,000 I'm going to
ask for next year." It's a good thing, too, because the following
year he was one of the league's worst in coming off the bench.

Be true to yourself, whoever you are.

The Giants acquired a truly multi-dimensional shortstop in 1984. Jose Gonzalez switched his name to Uribe Gonzalez before settling on Jose Uribe. His given name would do damage to any box score: Jose Altagracia Gonzalez Uribe.

82

The glass is half full.

It's an honor simply to pitch in an All-Star Game,
which Atlee Hammaker did in 1983.
Atlee entered the game in the third inning
and retired two of the batters he faced.

The glass is half empty— and just shattered in the shower.

Atlee Hammaker did not actually pitch in the All-Star Game as much as throw batting practice. He gave up the first grand slam (to Fred Lynn) in All-Star history and allowed seven runs in two-thirds of an inning.

Stop for a moment and
remember your first
Giants game.

Time is of the essence.

Time is of the essence. The shadow moves
From the plate to the box, from the box to second base,
From second to the outfield to the bleachers.

Time is of the essence. The crowd and players
Are the same age always, but the man in the crowd
Is older every season. Come on, play ball!
—Rolfe Humphries' *Polo Grounds*

Trot to the beat of your own drummer.

During the 1987 Playoffs, left fielder Jeffrey Leonard infuriated the opposition Cardinals, in part with his four home runs, but particularly with his flapdown, a home run trot with one arm tight to his side. Leonard was named the Series' MVP, which could have stood for Most Volatile Performer.

A little pain never hurt anyone.

"When I got to third base, I looked up and saw the team waiting for me," said Armando Rios after a game-winning, pinch-hit homer on July 18, 2000. "You see the team waiting for you, trying to pretty much beat you up when you get to home plate. It's a great feeling."

No matter what, keep swinging; something good might happen.

Ron Herbel was 0 for the 1964 season in 47 at bats.
He was 1 for 49 in 1965, 1 for 38 in 1966, and (Holy
Hornsby, Batman!) 3 for 28 in 1967.

Baseball is a game of pinches.

Entering the bottom of the ninth trailing Pittsburgh 11-1 on May 5, 1958, the Giants were in trouble until Bill Rigney sent up a parade of pinch-hitters. Three of them—Jimmy King, Johnny Antonelli, and Bob Speake—doubled in succession to help close the gap to 11-10. With the bases loaded and two outs, rookie Don Taussig stepped in for Antonelli—a pinch-hitter for a pinch-hitter—and popped up to second baseman Bill Mazeroski for the game's final out.

Political correctness exists for a reason.

Christy Mathewson recommended rubbing the heads of African-American children for luck. "I've walked…with ball-players," wrote Mathewson, "and seen them stop a young Negro and take off his hat and run their hands through his kinky hair. Then I've seen the same ball-player go out and get two or three hits… and play the game of his life."

Fight prejudice.

"Just give me a fungo stick and I'll lick all these bums myself." Cozy Dolan was referring to the Ku Klux Klan in Sarasota, Florida, in 1924 while the Giants were at training camp. The Klan marched outside the Giants' hotel to show their displeasure of sportswriters who had criticized the climate. Perhaps they wanted to know if the weather called for hoods.

Celebrate Color.

Vida Blue, Bud Black, Bill White, a multitude of
Browns (including Chris, Ollie, and Jumbo), David Green,
and Red Schoendienst have all worn Giants uniforms. Chief
Yellowhorse, sadly, did not.

Know your priorities— and follow them.

"'Scuse me, somebody important just came in."
—Toots Shor's dustoff of penicillin discoverer
Sir Alexander Fleming when slugging outfielder
Mel Ott arrived at Toots' restaurant

Anything is possible.

Mike Benjamin, who entered the 1995 season with
a career batting average of .186, got six hits in a game against
the Cubs and collected 14 hits over three games
to set a major league record.

Keep your work area clear of debris.

Not one, but two routine grounders hit pebbles and bounded over the head of third baseman Freddie Lindstrom in Game 7 of the 1924 World Series. The two bad hop singles gave the Washington Senators a 4-3 win for the championship.

If you feel sick,
go to work anyway.

Willie Mays nearly pulled himself from the lineup before an
April 30, 1961, game against the Milwaukee Braves
because he was ill, the result of a late-night snack.
Mays played and became the sixth player in history
to homer four times in a game.

"Give your friends names they can live up to. Throw your best pitches in the 'pinch.' Be humble and gentle and kind."

—Christy Mathewson

You're never too old…

In 1904, 11 years after he retired from baseball, Jim O'Rourke
returned at the age of 52 to play one game at catcher for
the New York Giants. He had one hit in four at bats, scored
a run, and gave pride to the aged everywhere.

...But age still matters.

As a 0-0 game entered extra innings, Juan Marichal, 25, was
asked if he was through for the day. "A 42-year-old man is
still pitching," said Marichal, referring to the Braves' Warren Spahn.
"I can't come out." Neither pitcher did, and Marichal
eventually won on a Willie Mays home run in the 16th inning.

Dress lightly or get stronger teammates.

"There isn't a person in this locker room
who can carry my jockstrap."
—Barry Bonds

Good things come to those who wait.

Moonlight Graham played in one major league game in
his career and never even got to bat. His break, however,
came some 85 years after his lone appearance when
Burt Lancaster portrayed him in *Field of Dreams*.
There is hope for all of us.

David D'Antonio played shortstop for the Giants, Orioles, Royals, and Pirates from 1968-1974. Unfortunately for him, those were the Giants, Orioles, Royals, and Pirates that competed in Little League and Pony League in Santa Clara, California.

The Giants Fan's Little Book of Wisdom is D'Antonio's second book. His first, *Invincible Summer*, was featured in *Sports Illustrated* and *The Sporting News*. The book followed the author's 5-month, 43-state, 26,000-mile, first-of-its-kind journey across America in search of the graves of baseball's greats.

Since birth, or at least since his first base hit, D'Antonio has been a die-hard Giants fan, a reason for optimism and patience, for there is always hope that every Johnny Rabb can turn into Johnny Bench, that this season, any season, can end with a mid-October victory.

D'Antonio lives with his wife Ann in San Leandro, California. A former journalist, he now teaches American History and English and coaches wrestling at Bancroft Middle School, where he practices his Marichal-esque high leg kick in the faculty room and still wonders how he can get his name into a major league box score.